THE FED WATCHER'S HANDBOOK

SIMULATING THE FEDERAL RESERVE'S FOMC IN CLASSROOMS AND ORGANIZATIONS

Anthony J. Pennings, PhD

ACKNOWLEDGMENTS

This work has been supported by the 2014 Hannam University, Linton School of Global Business, Republic of Korea Research Fund

DEDICATION

Mahalo to my family for their patience and support.

CONTENTS

Contents

1 Introduction

The Federal Reserve Bank is one of the most powerful institutions in the world. It is the chief determiner of the United States' monetary policy and is charged with the often competing goals of fostering sustainable economic growth, maximizing employment, and maintaining stable prices. The "Fed," as it is often called, can create money - a little by printing dollars - even less with coins - but a whole lot with a touch of a mouse! It monitors the economy and provides a broad range of financial reports. It also regulates banks throughout the US. Last, but not least, it provides an electronic network infrastructure for transferring money and clearing checks and other transactions.

The actions of the Fed can have an considerable impact on various private and public sector organizations. Big and small companies, as well as local municipalities, states, and the Federal government are impacted by a number of economic factors that the Fed can influence. These include the prices of goods and services, the cost of borrowing money, the rate of exchange for international currencies, and the general state of the economy. Not surprisingly, it makes sense for these organizations to monitor the actions of the Fed closely.

The Fed houses the Federal Open Market Committee (FOMC), which can set targets for the amount of money in the economy, as well as the interest rates for the cost of that money. The FOMC has the extraordinary capability to either create money to stimulate the economy, or absorb it from the banking system to avoid or reduce inflation. The twelve-person committee meets regularly to assess the state of the economy and make decisions that can influence the nation's money supply and its economy.

A case to consider was the financial crisis that began to take shape in 2007. A housing bubble emerged due to low interest rates and a global system of capital flows that channeled money into the selling of mortgages, based on the model of student loans. Banks and other financial institutions made the loans for home purchases and repackaged them into larger financial instruments that were then sold off to domestic and international investors. This resupplied the capital for more loans that expanded the credit and housing bubble. Tensions emerged as many homeowners fell behind on their payments. Banks, insurers, and mortgage firms started to fail in the spring of 2008, prompting a worldwide financial panic by the end of that year.

The FOMC, headed by former Fed Chairman Ben Bernanke, moved quickly to avert a possible deflationary meltdown of the economy that could have led to a major worldwide depression. In the years 2008-2013, the Fed virtually created trillions of dollars to help the US out what was called the "Great Recession." Through low interest rates and additional programs such as Quantitative Easing (QE), the FOMC injected massive amounts of money into the economy. While not everyone agreed with their policies and some feared runaway inflation, their actions slowly helped the economy, and particularly the stock markets.

While teaching economics at New York University, I developed a simulation of the Federal Reserve's Federal Open Market Committee for my undergraduate Macroeconomics class. I wanted a way to make the material more relevant for students and to give them real insights into how the economy worked, not just abstract models and dense vocabulary. Later I refined it for an MBA class in digital economics at St. Edwards University in Austin, Texas. The students helped me understand how the simulation was useful for startups and other organizations operating in the real world.

The exercise works really well in a semester timeframe as the FOMC usually meets two times during that period. The participants can conclude the simulation a day or two before the actual FOMC meets and compare their conclusions and policy suggestions. Unlike some of my colleagues at NYU, I have yet to receive a Nobel Prize for my economics work (I'm not holding my breath), but I am quite proud of the FOMC simulation and the impact it had on my students.

In the exercise, participants take on the roles of the key members of the FOMC, mainly the presidents of various Fed Districts and members of the Fed's Board of Governors. Each one studies the background of their assigned member and their responsibilities. They do economic research and participate in the decision-making on determining the interest rates that are so crucial to a modern economy. In the process, the participants not only learn significant economic principles, but use them throughout the course of the exercise. By acting in the capacity of an FOMC member they develop a greater appreciation for the complexities and impact of monetary policy on the general economy.

Serious Play

The simulation draws on the study of games and play as well as established education theory. In 2009, I had a chance to travel to Savannah, Georgia to present a paper on the topic for economics professors at the Annual Economics Teaching Conference.[1] I also did an extensive workshop that explained the educational rationale for the simulation.

I acknowledged the influence of *Rules of Play: Game Design Fundamentals* by Katie Salen Tekinbas and Eric Zimmerman. This classic in game theory helped me understand that simulations are representations of reality that can be structured to produce meaningful play and measurable outcomes.[2] In fact, I called the paper "Serious Play" because participants simulate real activities that have vital consequences for the lives of millions of people.

I also used the work of famous educational theorist Benjamin Bloom to discuss the value of the simulation.[3] He developed a framework for understanding educational activities and objectives that offer insights into the learning activities of the simulation and the results it produces. Bloom's model consists of three 'overlapping domains' that operate to make the simulation rewarding for the participants:

Cognitive – recall of information and basic intellectual skills;

Affective – patterns of attention, interest, interpersonal awareness, and the ability to take responsibility in interactions with others;

Psychomotor – physical skills that involve dexterity, vocalization, speed, fine motor skills and other attributes that influence performance-oriented actions.

As in most college-level courses, cognitive concerns are primary, but the simulation provides opportunities to reinforce and enhance other aspects of their learning as well. In Chapter 9, I list some of the benefits observed under each of Bloom's categories.

While it is too early to provide a definitive evaluation of the exercise, appraising its attributes and weaknesses within the context of its gameplay – its ability to produce meaningful experiences and outcomes - provides a starting point for further analysis and criteria for the evaluating the simulation.

Overview of the Book

This book details the objectives, logistics, and assessment of the FOMC simulation, a role-playing exercise in which the participants develop expertise in economic and monetary policy matters. It first provides a brief overview of money and fractional reserve banking. It then introduces the Federal Reserve Bank and the key role of the FOMC. It also describes the electronic trading activities that are used to influence the economy through the directives of the FOMC. Next, it describes the actual logistics of the simulation, including key assignments and their assessment. Lastly, the book provides a framework to understand and evaluate the dynamics of the FOMC simulation as an educational tool and a role-playing game.

My intention here is to create the opportunity for participants to explore the role of the Federal Reserve Bank and discuss its merits and its influence on the economy. This book is short because I do not want to do too much of the participant's work for them and deprive them of much of the value that can be gained from the exercise.

2 Understanding Money and Banking

Comprehending the basic roles of money, banking and monetary policy is useful to understand how the Fed works. First, it is important to understand that we live in a world where money is no longer directly connected to gold or silver, or any other physical asset for that matter. Money operates within a symbolic system in which currencies are issued by the government or its central banks (In the US, it's the Federal Reserve) and its value rests on the public's confidence that it can be exchanged for goods and services. Money is the product of a "social contract" in which we agree to:

-   Use it as a medium of exchange for buying and selling, and also for settling debts;

-   Express the value of goods and services in terms of a common unit of account, such as the US dollar;

-   Hold money as a store of value and for future use.

Society seems to want money to reconcile issues dealing with exchange and the estimation of value. Many things can operate as money. In post-World War II Germany, cigarettes and cognac served as currencies. The American military actively inserted these two items into the war-torn economy to facilitate the trade of food and other essentials until an official currency could be accepted.

Most people recognize that a bank is a useful place to keep your money. Less obvious is how banking, or what is called the fractional banking system, works. Banks hold a small amount of the money they get as deposits and lend out the rest. The Fed requires that they hold about 10 percent of their customer's deposits in reserve for liquidity and protection. These "required reserves" are stored in the form of paper money or coins stored in a bank's vaults or as deposits in their account with the Fed. These reserves allow the banks to serve customers who need cash and also assist the Fed in check clearing between banks. Legal reserves are defined by the Fed and can include marketable debt securities such as US Treasury bonds. Any amounts of legal reserves held by the banks over the required reserves are called excess reserves and are allowed to be loaned out again to businesses or consumers.

Ideally, much of the money they lend out will also be deposited back into the banking system – either by the borrower or someone from which the borrower purchased goods or services. Once again, a fraction is held in reserve, and the excess is lent out, including overnight to other banks through what is called the Fed Funds market. This virtual marketplace uses Fedwire, a real-time, electronic network that connects banks and allows them to lend reserves to each other overnight at interest rates guided by the FOMC.

Banks borrow money from each other through the Fed Funds market so they can expand their loan portfolios. If they determine they can make a profit by borrowing the money from other banks and lending it out at an advantageous rate, they will likely do that. Alternatively, they may decide that it is advantageous to hold interest-bearing bonds with their deposits rather than lend out the money. These profit calculations made by the banks form the rationale for the FOMC policy prescriptions and the trading operations they direct.

No doubt, fractional reserve banking is capitalism "with its foot to the floor" - to use an automobile metaphor. This process continuously creates new money for investment and innovation, but is in the form of debt and often leads to bankruptcies, bad credit, and heartbreak. The cycle accelerates what economists like Joseph Schumpeter and Werner Sombart called "creative destruction." This term refers to the constant pressure on businesses to innovate and improve their profitability, or experience default on their loans and face financial collapse. The belief here is that business failure clears the way for new forms of wealth creation. Companies like Blockbuster fail, and new companies like Netflix emerge with new ideas about getting that movie or TV show to you either by mailing a DVD or letting you stream the video over the Internet.

3 The Federal Reserve System

The Fed was created in the aftermath of a devastating financial crisis in 1907. Although the crisis was soon alleviated, primarily by the actions of the infamous New York banker JP Morgan, it drew public anger and calls for reform. Even the famous children's book *The Wonderful Wizard of Oz*, written a few years earlier by L. Frank Baum, is said to be an allegorical satire of the dysfunctional banking system of the time. In 1908, President Teddy Roosevelt pushed for the formation of a commission to study banking systems around the world. They concluded that the US system was inefficient and that the US dollar had little impact on world trade.

Many conspiracy theories surround the creation of the Federal Reserve System. Some say the Fed was created to replace J.P. Morgan, who was the most influential banker at the turn of the century. Others point to the secrecy of the meetings on Jekyll Island in Georgia where banking elites met to discuss new possibilities. But it is no secret that bank representatives worked with politicians over the next few years to draw up the new system of monetary control.

Legislation was eventually drafted by the US Congress and a few months after JP Morgan died, President Woodrow Wilson signed the *Federal Reserve Act of 1913*, otherwise known at the time as the "Currency Bill."

Like the central banks of other countries, the Federal Reserve provides financial services for the government and private banks, particularly through its Fedwire network. Fedwire is probably the most sophisticated and secure computer network in the world, transmitting some $3.5 trillion dollars a day.[4] Originally developed for check clearances, any large government or corporate payment will likely go through the Fedwire system.

The Fed also protects the banking system through regulation and by setting "reserve requirements." As mentioned before, the US banking system uses a fractional reserve system, meaning that banks hold a percentage of their deposits as reserves and lend out the rest as loans to the public. These reserves act as a partial insurance system, in case too many depositors want to withdraw funds from their accounts. They are backed up by the Federal Deposit Insurance Corporation (FDIC) that protects deposit accounts up to $250,000.

The Fed is run by a Board of Governors and its Chair, currently Janet Yellen. It is organized into 12 Federal Reserve District Banks representing different parts of the country. A large number of depository institutions are also considered part of the Federal Reserve System along with commercial banks, member banks, savings and loan associations, as well as credit unions.

The Fed can influence the amount of money in circulation by requiring banks to hold more money in reserve (holding cash in their vaults or in financial instruments at the Fed) although it rarely uses this option. It prefers instead to maintain a stable 10 percent reserve requirement and use other policy options to control the nation's money supply.

Since 2008, the Fed has been paying an interest rate paid on required and excess balances stored at Reserve Banks. The rate is determined by the Board and effectively gives the Fed an additional tool to conduct monetary policy.[5]

Another option they have to influence the money supply is by lending money directly to the banks at prescribed interest rates through what is called the discount rate. This option is also not preferred, although it has proved useful during certain periods when the Fed wanted to pump money quickly into the banking system. One example was the events of 9/11 when banks needed quick access to money to maintain stable operations.

The Fed's preferred method for controlling the money supply is through a system that has evolved over the last 50 years that influences the amount of money banks can lend to each other. This is called the Fed Funds Rate and is the major focus of the Fed's Federal Open Market Committee (FOMC) that will be discussed in more detail in the next section.

Recently, the Fed has used a set of programs known as Quantitative Easing or "QE" to insert money into the economy. This action involves buying non-Treasury financial assets, including mortgage-backed securities, from banks and other private financial institutions. Not only does this inject additional money, or "liquidity" into the economy but it lowers interest rates on these longer term instruments. The Fed turned to this approach because interbank interest rates in the Fed Funds market were already near zero, and they also wanted to boost the housing market by keeping mortgage interest rates low.

To review, the Fed has several tools to influence the amount of money in the economy:

- Reserve requirements
- Interest paid on required and excess reserves

- Discount rate

- Open market operations

- Quantitative easing

In the next section, we will look more closely at how the FOMC monitors the economy and how they attempt to control the amount of money in circulation by targeting interest rates through their open market operations.

4 Federal Open Market Committee (FOMC) and the Fed Funds Rate

As we saw in the previous section, the Federal Reserve controls the nation's monetary policy through several activities. Its primary tool for making adjustments in the economy is by targeting the interest rates of the Federal Funds Market and is coordinated by the FOMC. This is the rate that banks borrow from each other on an overnight basis via the Fedwire digital network.

Banks borrow through this system to increase their excess reserves and that allows them to lend out more money into the economy. If the Fed Funds Rate is high, banks are less likely to borrow money and consequently fewer bank reserves are available to lend out to their customers. This loss of "liquidity" will contract the money supply and thus reduce economic activity. On the other hand, if the Fed Funds Rate is low, banks have an incentive to borrow money and lend it out.

The banks make money by lending it out at higher rates than they borrow it. These interest rates will help determine what consumers and companies will pay for various loans such as credit cards, mortgages, participant loans, and for your car as well. The Fed does not have direct control over your loan amounts, but it can influence them. Another influence they have is on the amount the banks will pay for your savings CD rates, for example, have been at historic lows since the Fed Funds Rates decreased. One more reason to invest elsewhere.

And a last note, the Fed Funds Rate is not to be confused with the Prime Rate, which is the interest rate loosely decided by a consensus of the largest banks and is only offered to their best customers. A widely quoted prime rate figure is produced by the *Wall Street Journal* that surveys the 30 largest banks while the Federal Reserve posts its own prime rate based on a survey of the top 25 banks. Still, it is the benchmark rate for determining other loans and is based on the Fed Funds Rate.

The next two sections explore the FOMC and its activities in more depth. Chapter 5 assists the simulation by identifying the members of the FOMC, where they are from, and what they do in the crucial meetings that determine interest rates and other aspects of monetary policy. Chapter 6 explores the mechanics of the open market operations that carry out the FOMC's target instructions. This is when traders at the New York Federal Reserve Bank actively buy and sell government bonds, and sometimes other marketable securities, to influence the amount of money in the banking system.

A very important logic unfolds when the Fed's traders get on their computers and engage in this trading process. When they buy government bonds from the banks, they inject money into the economy. Likewise, when Fed traders sell bonds, they suck money out of the economy. Chapter 6 then explores the impact this process has on the Fed Funds Rate and interest rates throughout the economy. It is important that participants in the simulation understand this part intuitively. But don't worry, that is what the simulation is designed to do.

5 Who Makes Up the Federal Open Market Committee?

The Chair leads the 12 member group. Seven members of the Board of Governors of the Federal Reserve System are ongoing members. One of the BOG members serves as Vice-Chair. Current Chair Janet Yellen was the Vice-Chair under Ben Bernanke. The President of the Federal Reserve Bank of New York is always included in the FOMC because of the key role of their trading operations and international activities. Four additional members are drawn from the remaining eleven Reserve Bank Presidents on a rotating basis. Each must represent one the following four groupings, representing different parts of the country.

Group 1 - Boston, Philadelphia, and Richmond;

Group 2 - Cleveland and Chicago;

Group 3 - Atlanta, St. Louis, and Dallas;

Group 4 - Minneapolis, Kansas City, and San Francisco.

This diversification ensures that different parts of the country have a voice in the FOMC decisions. Non-voting Presidents usually participate in the FOMC meetings but don't have voting privileges. Note: In the FOMC simulation, more Reserve Bank Presidents can be used than the official amount.

The 2015 Members of the FOMC are listed below.[6]

Members

Janet L. Yellen, Board of Governors, Chair
William C. Dudley, New York, Vice Chairman
Lael Brainard, Board of Governors
Charles L. Evans, Chicago
Stanley Fischer, Board of Governors
Jeffrey M. Lacker, Richmond
Dennis P. Lockhart, Atlanta
Jerome H. Powell, Board of Governors
Daniel K. Tarullo, Board of Governors
John C. Williams, San Francisco

Alternate Members

James Bullard, St. Louis
Esther L. George, Kansas City
Loretta J. Mester, Cleveland
Eric Rosengren, Boston
Christine M. Cumming, First Vice President, New York

The FOMC generally meet eight times throughout the year to make decisions on monetary policy and publish valuable information on the economy. Although only required to hold four meetings a year, the FOMC generally meet every eight weeks.

The meetings are usually held at the Eccles Federal Reserve Board Building, named after Marriner S. Eccles, a former Chairman of the Federal Reserve. It is located on Constitution

Avenue in Washington D.C. and was completed in 1937 and dedicated by President Franklin Delano Roosevelt that same year.

They start off with economic presentations by the NY Fed's Manager of the System Open Market Account and the Director of Research and Statistics at the Board. These presentations are followed by two "Go-Rounds". In the first, the District Bank Presidents present on the economic conditions in their respective districts. Then the Director of Monetary Affairs, who acts as the FOMC Secretary, draws on the Fed's "Teal Book" (historically the Blue Book until 2010) to overview key economic data and lay out different policy options.

After the presentations, the Chair puts forward a policy prescription, primarily a target for the Fed Funds interest rate. Usually, intensive discussion and lobbying occurs beforehand to make sure dissenting issues are addressed and that a unanimous decision is reached.

After the votes are tallied, and the meeting adjourned, a press release is distributed to announce the results of the meeting. This document is carefully worded with an eye to how it might impact various financial markets. The FOMC also produces a more technical directive that instructs the New York Federal Reserve Bank to carry out its policy prescription for the nation's money supply. High tech trading operations and expertise are located in downtown Manhattan to influence the Fed Funds Market and guide its interest rates.

Minutes of the FOMC meeting are published three weeks after the conclusion of each FOMC meeting, but complete transcripts are held for five years after the meeting before they are published.

6 Fed Open Market Operations

The FOMC does not set the rate of interest, but rather it sets a target that actual trading operations are instructed to meet. They do this by instructing their in-house traders to buy or sell US Treasury bonds to influence the money and credit conditions in the economy. These are known as the Open Market Operations (OMO) and they are located at the New York Fed.

Workday mornings, around 9:30 AM, with the exact time of intervention determined by chance, the traders at the OMO intervene to influence the Fed Funds Market. They get on their computers and guide the Fed Funds Rate towards the FOMC's target for interest rates. They operate according to basic supply and demand principles. It helps that the Fed has a lot of financial power to entice banks to buy or sell their holdings of government bonds. Let's look from the banks' perspective.

Banks borrow money from each other through the Fed Funds Market so they can increase their lending to households or businesses. The Fed Funds system gives them the opportunity to borrow the excess reserves from other banks if they want to make more loans. On the other hand, if the price is right, they may decide to lend their excess reserves overnight. Banks may also decide to buy government interest-bearing bonds with their excess reserves rather than lend out the money. This would leave them with less excess money to lend out to other banks.

The traders buy or sell government securities through the OMO to influence the banking system's lending behavior, but it would be a mistake to think that the OMO trade directly in the federal funds market. Instead, Fed traders deal with a group of private financial firms called the primary dealers.

The OMO conducts trading operations that both hold debt for long periods and also for short-term operations using repurchase agreements with maturities of less than a week. They trade with roughly 22 primary dealers that act as intermediaries with the larger banking system.

Primary dealers have a relationship with the Fed as trading counterparties that requires them to abide my certain rules. They are required to participate in government auctions of US Treasury securities (T-bills, T-notes, and T-bonds). They are required to make bids or offers when the Fed conducts its open market operations. They are also required to supply the Fed OMO with information about the market conditions for these debt instruments.[7] Many of the primary dealers are financial firms based in other countries are required to sell or buy around the world. In sum, primary dealers are required to "make markets." This means acquiring an inventory and being willing to fill orders for a particular security at quoted bid and ask prices. In other words, if a bank wants to buy or sell their T-bills, the primary dealer is available to make that transaction, at market prices.

In 2008, the credit and housing crisis sent the US into an economic recession and had an impact on the primary dealers. The collapse of Bear Sterns, Countrywide Securities, and Lehman Brothers temporarily reduced the total by three and MF Global was removed in 2011. At other times, the list has increased to over 40, as it did in the late 1980s.

In February 2014, according to the Federal Reserve Bank of New York, the list included:

Bank of Nova Scotia, New York Agency
BMO Capital Markets Corp.
BNP Paribas Securities Corp.
Barclays Capital Inc.
Cantor Fitzgerald & Co.
Citigroup Global Markets Inc.
Credit Suisse Securities (USA) LLC
Daiwa Capital Markets America Inc.
Deutsche Bank Securities Inc.
Goldman, Sachs & Co.
HSBC Securities (USA) Inc.
Jefferies LLC
J.P. Morgan Securities LLC
Merrill Lynch, Pierce, Fenner & Smith Incorporated
Mizuho Securities USA Inc.
Morgan Stanley & Co. LLC
Nomura Securities International, Inc.
RBC Capital Markets, LLC
RBS Securities Inc.
SG Americas Securities, LLC
TD Securities (USA) LLC
UBS Securities LLC.[8]

If the Fed's OMO purchase bonds from the primary dealers, it will inject money into the banking system and decrease the incentive to borrow from the Fed Funds Market, consequently reducing interest rates. If they sell bonds through the primary dealers, it will absorb money from the banks and increase the incentive to borrow through the Fed Fund Market and thus increase interest rates. So the result is that trading operations directly increase or decrease the level of Fed balances, not the flow of federal funds transactions among banks.[9]

The buying and selling of U.S. government securities from these primary dealers influence the price of money bankers are lending to each other overnight. If the Fed purchases bonds it will increase bank reserves and decrease the Fed Funds interest rate. If they sell bonds to the primary dealers, it will draw money out of bank reserves and increase the Fed Funds interest rate. By making it attractive for banks to buy government securities from them, the Fed can "tighten" the money supply; conversely, the purchase of bonds will inject money into the economy.

It is this inverse relationship between OMO trades and the Fed Funds Rate that guides the nation's money supply. If bank reserves increase because the banks have sold their government bonds to the Fed, the prices of interest rates, the amount lenders will charge for borrowing that money, will decrease. Likewise, if bank reserves fall because banks prefer to use that money to buy interest-bearing government bonds from the Fed, that action will increase the Fed Funds rate and an increase in interest rates throughout the economy will likely occur.

Remember these formulas:

– Fed Purchases • Increases Bank Reserves • Decreases Fed Funds Rate • Interest Rates Fall

– Fed Sells • Decreases Bank Reserves • Increases Fed Funds Rate • Interest Rates Increase

7 The FOMC Simulation

In this section, I describe how a class or an organization can simulate the FOMC activities in a way that engages participants or employees. The simulation presents many opportunities to learn about how the Federal Reserve works and how it influences the economy. As most of my experience with the simulation has been in the classroom, I will first describe the educational objectives of simulation and then the mechanics of how it works with an introductory economics class.

The main objectives of the FOMC Simulation are:

• Understand the functions and role of money in the economy

• Comprehend the role of fractional reserve banking in the US society

• Recognize the primary policy tools available to the Federal Reserve to influence the money supply

• Understand how the FOMC targets interest rates through its open market operations

• Recognize the value and limitations of national accounting measurements for understanding economic conditions

• Develop an understanding of what causes economic growth

• Learn how inflation and deflation emerge within the economy

• Grasp the implications of government spending and fiscal policy on Fed policy

• Understand the relationship between FOMC actions and the value of the US dollar

• Learn the distinction between "printing" money and increasing the money supply (and how the money supply can be decreased).

In the classroom simulation, groups of 8-15 participants take on the roles of individual FOMC members, do research on their responsibilities and participate in meetings similar to the actual FOMC meeting.

The exercise starts on the first day of class when the overview of the course is presented and covers the length of the semester. One, two or even three meetings are scheduled, depending on the length of the semester.

The meetings are conducted just before an actual FOMC meeting so the participants can compare their results with the announcements from the Fed. It is best to organize around a large table or get into a circle. Several tasks assess the participant's progress and overall learning.

The roles taken on by the participants are usually determined by lottery. One simple way is with the names of each member of the FOMC and their position written on a piece of paper and literally drawn out a hat or box. For instance, *Janet Yellen, Chair* would be on one of the slips of paper.

A significant change from the actual FOMC meeting participation is that it is best for the participants to be primarily District Bank Presidents. This position has a clearer set of responsibilities and allows the participants to research as much of the US economic geography as possible. In a case where a participant becomes a Board of Governor, a specific task like covering an industry (auto, high tech, energy) is preferred. This choice is often based on a Governor's interest. For example, Dr. Lael Brainard, has expertise in global economic challenges and her participant "alter ego" might report on trade imbalances or currency exchange rates.

Just as in the actual FOMC meeting, the New York Fed President is always in attendance. The NY Fed Vice-President is a good choice for a participant if the class number exceeds the number of Bank Presidents. She/he can report on the operations of the open market trading desks.

While a regular economics curriculum should be followed, one rather controversial change is suggested. Lectures on money, banking, and monetary policy should be presented up front, in the first few modules of the class. The traditional macroeconomic textbook usually has these topics near the end. Instead, chapters dealing with money and its functions - liquidity, monetary aggregates M1, M2, the fractional banking system, the role of central banks, and monetary policy should be covered quite early. This change is recommended to prepare thoroughly for the simulation. In an organization doing the simulation, participants might take turns presenting this type of information.

Moving money topics to the forefront works surprisingly well as it is very tangible for participants. Monetary policy is a bit more challenging, but most participants have heard of the Federal Reserve and the mystical "interest rates" that are announced prominently on the news eight times a year. The chapters dealing with supply and demand are also important for students to understand the market logic involved with OMO trading activities. By the time of the first meeting, 7 or 8 chapters of a traditional macroeconomics textbook can be covered.

The simulation runs throughout the semester and does not always involve learning a progression of economic ideas. Rather it forms a set of core tasks around which participants gather knowledge and attach ideas from the study of other issues such Gross Domestic Product (GDP) and fiscal policy.

Participants present bios of their "alter egos" two or three weeks after the start of the course. They research the work background, previous job positions, education, and authored articles and books of their assigned FOMC member. Personal information such as hobbies, family status, and other interests are also pursued to help humanize the FOMC members, often bankers with financially esoteric backgrounds. Then, in the first group activity, they read a one-page report to the group and turn it in to be marked for credit.

The bios help the participants identify with their alternative personalities. It should be noted however that the goal is not for participants to remain "in character" very long but rather transition to seeing themselves as an FOMC member with their own educated opinions. This somewhat bifurcated consciousness is not that difficult to obtain and allows the participant to develop more confidence in their individual knowledge and abilities.

After presenting the bios of their respective FOMC members, the participants begin research for the first FOMC meeting.

Participants are required to find and follow several (3-5) major online newspapers from their respective districts. Each district usually has several branches. For example, the Sixth District, headquartered in Atlanta, has branches in Birmingham, Jacksonville, Miami, Nashville, and New Orleans. It is advisable to identify these branches and follow important news sources from each area.

Another important resource is The Federal Reserve "Beige Book," known officially as the Summary of Commentary on Current Economic Conditions by Federal Reserve District. It is published 7-10 days before the FOMC meeting and is available on their website.

The Beige Book is prepared eight times a year and contains anecdotes, statistical data and economic analysis from each Fed district. The real FOMC members often cite it. Some criticize it for not being scientific enough and the Fed website contains the following caveat: "This document summarizes comments received from business and other contacts outside the Federal Reserve System and is not a commentary on the views of Federal Reserve officials." Still, it particularly useful for the participants' research as it presents relevant information in a comprehensible format and language.

It gathers the information under the following general headings:

Consumer Spending

Natural Resources and Agriculture

Energy and Mining

Employment, Wages, and Prices

Temporary Employment

Banking and Finance

Manufacturing and Transportation

Services

Retail Sales

Real Estate and Construction

The participants are expected to cover most of these topics while emphasizing aspects most relevant to their respective areas. For example, a report from the San Francisco would emphasize the high technology industries. The Richmond summary often emphasizes ports. A District President from Dallas would be expected to give significant insight regarding the energy sector.

The inherent danger of the Beige Report is that it is rather easy for participants to find relevant data. Consequently, they should be incentivized to do other research first through newspapers and journals. A limit to the exercise though is the tight time frame and the importance of having timely data for the FOMC meeting. Therefore, the use of the Beige Book is recommended despite the potential pitfalls.

8 Simulation Organization – The Meeting and Assessment

The Chair convenes the meeting and guides the process. The simulation, like the actual FOMC meeting, consists of two "go-rounds." In the simulation she/he starts the first round by briefly introducing key national economic data (US dollar, employment, gold, stock indexes, GDP, key energy prices). The Chair does not have a specific geographical or industry sector to cover so this gives him or her an overall perspective and helps them determine a strategy for the voting later.

Next, the District Bank Presidents and Board of Governors take turns presenting on their respective areas. The Chair introduces each as they present in alphabetical order. The presentations need to be written out (one page) and read aloud. They should not take longer than 5 minutes each. They should be sure to introduce themselves and their districts/areas in the beginning.

All the presentations should follow a standard set of categories. This could be alphabetical order: Agriculture, Banking and Finance, Consumer Spending, Employment, Housing, Natural Resources, Manufacturing, Real Estate, Retail, Services, and Transportation. A standard format will make it easier for the others to follow and force participants to vary from the Beige Book. It also helps later in assessing the participant's quality of research.

They should describe demographic and economic aspects of the district, noting key industries, resources, and sources of employment. Natural or economic events such as droughts, floods, and major bankruptcies should be mentioned. The economic effects of Hurricane Katrina in New Orleans was a major topic for the Atlanta Fed District in 2005.

If the class has more than 12 participants, some of them will be will not be Fed District Presidents. Others can be members of the Board of Governors. As mentioned above, Fed Governors do not have a geographical jurisdiction. Students should find out if they have an interest they can report on such as inflation/deflation, unemployment, or an industry such as automobile manufacturing, high tech, energy, etc. In larger classes, some participants have even taken on the personas of Congress or Cabinet members.

In the second "go-round," the Chair starts off by recommending a policy directive. This is usually an interest rate target, but they have even included a QE rate or a discount rate change. Each participant then gets a chance to express their views in support or opposition to the Chair's policy suggestion. Finally, voting commences, and the results tallied.

The Press Release

The final part of the simulated meeting can be the most difficult but is equally important. At this final stage, the Chair leads the group in the writing of the press release. Practically, it is useful to have the latest FOMC press release available for guidance and a computer with a projection system. The

FOMC press release is generally organized with an explanation of the FOMC's view of the economy first. Then in the second paragraph, a statement on price stability and whether they forecast inflation, deflation or stable prices is issued. Next, the policy directive is laid out. Finally, the voting for the policy prescription is listed with the names of the people voting with or against the consensus or abstaining from the vote.

The Final Assignment

After the simulation, each participant submits an assignment called the Fed Summary and Analysis. This report is usually about 10-12 pages and overviews the entire simulation.

The first part introduces the exercise and their role in it. Participants insert their bio report here as well. In the next section, the participant discusses what they learned in the simulation about the Federal Reserve Bank. For instance, how does the FOMC develop monetary policy and how do the traders at the New York Fed OMO carry out their directives? Did the participant really learn how the Fed guides the Fed Funds Rate? This section is usually 3-4 pages.

Next, they describe the economic situations in their district, including a description of the major economic drivers. With the insertion of their presentations, this section should be about 4-5 pages. Participants also need to present the evidence they used to suggest that interest rates should be lowered/raised?

Finally, they need to report on how the policy outcomes of the simulation mirrored or differed from the actual FOMC meeting that came after the simulation. Simulation learning can also be assessed with a multiple-choice exam or another testing instrument to determine if the participants understood key concepts. Students could also be asked to write about issues dealing with Fed and the gold standard, or even if the Fed should be replaced by computers as famed economist Milton Friedman has suggested.

While participants often find the Federal Reserve simulation obscure at first, they mostly come to find it an intriguing challenge that leads to substantial illuminations about the economy. The participants find an immediate connection to current economic developments. They also get relevant feedback from monitoring the Fed's actions and comparing it with their own, albeit simulated, opinions. The meetings present an opportunity to showcase research as well as engage in lively discussion.

9 Digital Media and Other Firms Using the Simulation

Initially developed for undergraduate students, I later applied the Fed simulation in an MBA course focused on digital media firms. The program was in Austin, Texas and consequently, I felt a burden to relate the Fed's actions to a variety of start-ups and tech companies.[10] In this chapter, I identify key components of the larger economy that digital media and even non-media companies should be watching. These companies should be aware of how decisions by the Federal Reserve can influence aspects of the economy – and ultimately their organizations.

Producers of digital goods and services need to develop educated expectations about economic conditions influencing their businesses. They need to tie observations about the economy and where it is heading to their decisions about hiring, production schedules, and investments in permanent facilities like studios or office space. While the Fed's actions, policies, and research are not the only points of concern that can impact a digital firm; they are significantly consequential to warrant sustained observation.

How do digital media managers conceptualize larger business trends and track this information while necessarily micromanaging the daily activities of their organizations? One of our media economics textbooks proved helpful. *The Economics and Financing of Media Companies* by Robert G. Picard pointed out four important areas where media companies should direct their attention:

the business cycle

inflation/deflation of prices

interest rates

and exchange rates

Although Picard barely mentions the Federal Reserve, we can address the above concerns, starting with the recurring and irregular expansions and contractions of economic activity known as the business cycle.[11]

The Federal Reserve influences the **business cycle** by controlling the supply of money in the economy. By injecting more money into the financial system, the FOMC can lower interest rates and consequently increase business investments and consumer spending. Economic growth means more jobs, increased incomes and more disposable income for consumers to spend. Sales of media products and services are subject to consumer incomes and expectations about the state of the economy. Monitoring the contraction and expansion of the economy supplies vital information about consumer spending patterns and confidence.

Media goods like game consoles and HDTVs are particularly sensitive to economic fluctuations. Advertising, a key driver of media sales, has been particularly sensitive to business conditions. But admittedly, more research needs to be done on digital media products as substitute goods for other entertainment pastimes, particularly in times of economic downturn. For example, films and radio were popular pastimes during the Great Depression as a means of escaping the harsh conditions of the time. More recently, Netflix began its historic rise during the "Great Recession." Video gaming also did well as consumers purchased relatively cheaper forms of entertainment that allowed them to stay home or take advantage of mobile leisure time.

Inflation can come either from too much money/demand in the economy or too few goods and services. If the economy is growing fast, prices for goods and wages increase accordingly. When prices inflate, it can be good for the economy as purchases are made more quickly to avoid the higher prices. Another incentive to consume is that the value of savings depreciates faster. Inflation is good for borrowers as they wind up spending less to pay off their debt. On the other hand, prolonged inflation makes it hard for producers to plan. Also, inventories can dry up as consumers hoard goods, contributing to shortages. Excessive inflation can be quite stressful for an economy as the US discovered during a period during the 1970s known as "stagflation," when the economy stagnated while experiencing high rates of inflation.

Deflation comes from too little money or "effective" demand, or an abundance of goods and services. Deflation has been a more persistent problem in our contemporary economy. Deflation has occurred despite the massive infusions of money into the economy by the Fed and through government spending.

While deflation mainly results from a slow economy and lack of demand, one of the reasons for our current deflationary trend has been the increasing efficiencies of digital products. This phenomenon follows Moore's Law that that predicts the speed of digital microprocessing doubles every 18 months. Digital technologies are allowing us "to do more with less" – including fewer human workers - contributing to lower wages.

Another issue is that while production and post-production expenditures costs are often high for digital products, efficient forms of delivery drive down what economists call "marginal costs." In general, the costs of producing an additional media item like a DVD is not very significant, as are the costs of printing one more book, or reaching an additional radio listener or television viewer. The efficiencies of digital distribution and delivery are driving down the costs of media content.

Competitive pressures due to low barriers to entry for Internet commerce has also pushed prices down.

Price stability is a major concern for the Federal Reserve, and they watch changes in prices closely.

Interest rates are the prime vehicle for the Federal Reserve to influence the price of money and consequently the supply of it in the economy. The cost of borrowing capital is critical for many digital media firms that need funds for new initiatives, expanding operations, or just cash flow for meeting payroll and other expenses. The Federal Reserve conducts complex financial trading operations to meet their target for interest rates that they announce about eight times a year following their two-day FOMC meetings.

With the globalization of the net-centric commercial activities, **exchange rates** are also a concern for digital media firms. The Fed rarely intervenes in the currency spot markets as exchange rate policy is the responsibility of the US Treasury. However, because global currency markets trade trillions of dollar each day; the New York Fed sometimes coordinates with the Treasury. Even then, it is more to signal a policy that can influence exchange rates, rather than to implement one.

The Fed can have an influence on exchange rates with their interest rate policy. Lower interest rates depress the value of the US dollar by discouraging purchases of U.S dollar denominated financial instruments. It also makes it attractive to borrow cheap US money and spend it internationally. Sending money offshore requires purchasing other currencies and that depresses the value of the US dollar. A cheap currency makes exporting goods and services more attractive but can drive up the prices of imports, including raw materials and other components needed for your own production processes.

10 Concluding Thoughts: Learning and Meaningful Play in the FOMC Simulation

In *Rules of Play: Game Design Fundamentals*, Salen Tekinbas and Zimmerman highlight the importance of significant interaction for developing a wide range of compelling games, simulations, and role-playing experiences. They argue that good games produce "meaningful play" for its participants and point to the relationship between player actions and the outcomes that result in successful game experiences. In the FOMC simulation, participants engage in a series of activities that lead to a system outcome, the policy directive.

Serious play is created when the relationships between participant action and outcomes are "both discernable and integrated into the larger context of the game...," in this case, the simulation. Each activity provides layers of understanding that accumulate and shape the participant's experience of the simulation. Taking on the role of a FOMC member, reporting on the economic conditions of an actual US Fed district, discussing the proposed directive, participating in the vote, and finally creating the press release, provides an equal opportunity for each participant to build their confidence and knowledge. Each individual's actions are woven into the total experience and adds to each step, finally leading to the final result. While it may be difficult for one individual FOMC member to influence the final policy decision, strong dissenting opinions can be registered in the press release.

It helps that the actual FOMC meets shortly after, so the group can compare their conclusions and policy directives with the real thing. By that time participants are fully conversant in the process and the implications of the FOMC policy decisions. Some of the best games are those that act out serious activities in non-threatening ways - and what could be more significant than making decisions that involve trillions of dollars and millions of jobs?

The concept of meaningful play, while evasive at times, provides a useful framework and a set of criteria for analyzing the effectiveness of the FOMC simulation. Appraising the simulation's attributes and weaknesses within the context of its gameplay – its ability to produce meaningful experiences and outcomes – provides a starting point for the evaluating the simulation.

Combined with Bloom's taxonomy, the concept of gameplay suggests that one way of understanding human learning is to conceive it as a progression of challenges leading to a set of integrated outcomes. Bloom's model provides additional ways we can discern learning outcomes, particularly if we examine his three 'overlapping domains:' the Cognitive – the recall of information and basic intellectual skills; the Affective – patterns of attention, interest, interpersonal awareness, and the ability to take responsibility in interactions with others; and the Psychomotor – physical skills that involve dexterity, speed, verbal acuity, fine motor skills and other attributes that influence performance-oriented actions.

Some of the related observations and feedback from the FOMC simulation are listed under each of Bloom's domains:

1. Cognitive domain (intellectual capability, i.e., knowledge, or 'think') • Decipher economic statistics and re-state data in one's own words, • Grasp the economic strengths and weaknesses of different parts of the US. • Translate economic data into policy decisions • Develop judgment related to economic markets • Reproduce key geo-industry issues • Conceptualize a press release

2. Affective domain (feelings, emotions and behavior, ie., attitude, or 'feel') • Anticipates the role of the Fed in the financial markets • Taking on the roles of District bank presidents • Enter into the imaginative realm of District Bank Presidents • Imitate the actions of a FOMC member, integrating expertise with statistical data

3. Psychomotor domain (manual and physical skills, ie., skills, or 'do') • Actively listen to others present complex data • Articulate data-based arguments • Imitate professional actions • Express meaningful interpretation • Develop oral precision in presenting economic arguments • Research and discover relevant economic data

The FOMC Simulation is designed to provide students and other participants with a powerful learning experience that helps them understand important aspects of the economy through a meaningful and interactive group experience. By taking on the persona of an FOMC member, they participate in a role-playing scenario based on actual real-life economic data and financial news. They research and report on key economic data in their assigned geographical area and participate in decision-making activities that mirror the actual Federal Reserve process.

The simulation reinforces important conceptual aspects of money, monetary policy and other macroeconomic principles while enhancing logical and emotive skills. Over the course of a few weeks or months, the participants address number of important economic and financial issues. These include understanding the causes of economic growth, the dynamics of the fractional reserve banking system, sources of inflation and deflation, the importance of national income measures, and the relationship between government spending and monetary policy. They grasp the logic of supply and demand and the economic power of large institutions.

Participants face a number of intellectual and emotional intelligence challenges as the simulation progresses. Each activity can provide cognitive, affective and psychomotor growth while helping them achieve the objectives of an economics class or an understanding of how the Fed influences their business firm or non-profit organization.

Whatever you think about the Federal Reserve, it is central to our current financial environment. Very few people understand the processes of the central bank or the impact it can have on the economy. Others fear the Fed and the power it has over the economy. In any case, it is important for people to come to grips with this important institution and the way it structures our current economy.

---

[1] Pennings, A.J. "Serious Play: Simulating the Fed's FOMC in the Classroom." Presentation/Paper Prepared for the Fifth Annual Economics

Teaching Conference. Savannah, Georgia, November 5-6. 2009.
[2] This understanding is combined from several parts of Katie Salen
Tekinbas and Eric Zimmerman. *Rules of Play: Game Design Fundamentals*.
Cambridge, MA: MIT, 2003. Print.
[3] Bloom, Benjamin S., et. al. (1956). *Taxonomy of Educational Objectives*,
New York: David McKay Company, Inc.
[4] In 2014, Fedwire processed some 135 million transactions totaling over
US$885 trillion dollars or $3.5 trillion dollars a day. That is certainly a lot
of money. Will Fedwire process a quadrillion US dollars in 2015?
[5] Changes in interest payment for reserves from
http://www.federalreserve.gov/monetarypolicy/reqresbalances.htm
[6] List of 2015 FOMC members from "Federal Open Market Committee."
FRB:. N.p., n.d. Web. 30 Mar. 2015.
[7] Primary dealer requirements from
http://www.ny.frb.org/markets/pridealers_policies.html
[8] "Primary Dealers List - Federal Reserve Bank of New York." Primary
Dealers List - Federal Reserve Bank of New York. N.p., n.d. Web. 31 Mar.
2015. http://www.newyorkfed.org/markets/pridealers_current.html
[9] Anthony J. Pennings, PhD. "The Fedwire Network and Open Market
Operations of the Federal Reserve" :. N.p., n.d. Web. 31 Mar. 2015.
[10] Thanks to Russell Rains, Gregg Perry, David Altounian and all the
DMBA students at St. Edward's University in Austin, Texas for a great
experience.
[11] Pennings, Anthony J., PhD. "Why Digital Media Firms Need to Fed
Watchers."*Why Digital Media Firms Need to Be Fed Watchers* :. N.p., 12
Dec. 2013. Web. 20 Apr. 2015. <http://apennings.com/media-
strategies/why-digital-media-firms-need-to-be-fed-watchers/>.